Supporting Childrer

Cerebral Palsy

Hull Learning Services

David Fulton Publishers Ltd
The Chiswick Centre, 414 Chiswick High Road, London W4 5TF

www.fultonpublishers.co.uk
www.onestopeducation.co.uk

First published in Great Britain by Hull Learning Services

David Fulton Publishers is a division of Granada Learning Limited, part of ITV plc.

British Library Cataloguing in Publication Data
A catalogue record for this book is available from the British Library.

ISBN 1 84312 220 0

Contents

Foreword

This book was produced in partnership with the following services based in Hull:
- the Special Educational Needs Support Service (SENSS);
- the Education Service for Physical Disability (ESPD) and list;
- the Hull and District Cerebral Palsy Society.

It was written by:
> Jenny Fisher (ESPD)
> Elizabeth Morling (SENSS)
> Francesca Murray (Hull and District Cerebral Palsy Society).

It is one of a series of eleven titles providing an up-to-date overview of special educational needs for SENCOs, teachers and other professionals and parents.

The books were produced in response to training and information needs raised by teachers, support staff and parents in Hull. The aim of these books is to raise awareness and address many of the issues involved in creating inclusive environments.

For details of other titles and how to order, please go to: www.fultonpublishers.co.uk, or telephone: 0500 618052.

Introduction

A minority of pupils with cerebral palsy are educated in special schools. However, the inclusive agenda means that pupils who have cerebral palsy are, for the most part, educated in mainstream schools. The condition is such that pupils can usually access the full curriculum.

Inclusion in education

In order to understand the issues of cerebral palsy within the framework of the inclusion agenda, the following statements should be taken into consideration:

- Inclusion is recognising that all children have different abilities and experience and seeks to value and gain from those differences. It is not about expecting or trying to make everyone the same or behave in the same way.

- Inclusion in education involves the process of increasing the participation of students in, and reducing their exclusion from, the cultures, curricula and communities of local schools.

- Inclusion involves restructuring the cultures, policies and practices in schools so that they respond to the diversity of students in their locality.

- Inclusion is concerned with the learning and participation of all students vulnerable to exclusionary pressures, not only those with impairments or those who are categorised as having 'special educational needs'.

- Inclusion is concerned with improving schools for staff as well as for students.

- A concern with overcoming barriers to the access and participation of particular students may reveal gaps in the attempts of a school to respond to diversity more generally.

- All students have a right to an education in their locality.

- Diversity is not viewed as a problem to overcome, but as a rich resource to support the learning of all.

- Inclusion is concerned with fostering mutually sustainable relationships between schools and communities.

- Inclusion in education is one aspect of inclusion in society (Index for Inclusion).

"Education is vital to the creation of a fully inclusive society, a society in which all members see themselves as valued for the contribution they make. We owe all children – whatever their particular needs and circumstances, the opportunity to develop to their full potential, to contribute economically, and to play a full part as active citizens". David Blunkett

An inclusive culture is one in which:

- everyone is made to feel welcome;

- students help each other;

- staff collaborate with each other;

- staff and students treat one another with respect;

- there is a partnership between staff and parents/carers;

- all local communities are involved with the school;

- staff and governors work well together.

Inclusive values are established when:

- there are high expectations of all students;

- everyone shares a philosophy of inclusion;

- students are equally valued;

- staff and students are treated as human beings as well as occupants of a 'role';

- staff seek to remove all barriers to learning and participation in school;

- the school strives to minimise discriminatory practices.

Implications of the Disability Discrimination Act 1995 as amended by the SEN and Disability Act 2001

Part one of the Act

- strengthens the rights of children to be educated in mainstream schools;
- requires LEAs to arrange for parents and/or children with SEN to be provided with advice on SEN matters, and also a means of settling disputes with schools and LEAs (parent partnership services and mediation schemes);
- requires schools to tell parents where they are making special educational provision for their child and allows schools to request a statutory assessment of a pupil's needs.

In accordance with the above Act

LEAs and schools must:

- not treat disabled pupils less favourably;
- make reasonable adjustments so that the physical, sensory and learning needs of disabled pupils are accommodated, in order that they are not put at a substantial disadvantage to pupils who are not disabled;
- plan strategically and make progress in increasing not only physical accessibility to the schools' premises and to the curriculum, but also to improve the delivery of written information in an accessible way to disabled pupils (i.e. access to the curriculum via oral means, as well as the written word).

Definition of disability

- The Disability Discrimination Act uses a very broad definition of 'disability'. A person has a disability if he or she has a physical or mental impairment that has a substantial and long-term adverse effect on his or her ability to carry out normal day-to-day activities.
- The DDA definition of disability covers physical disabilities, sensory impairments, such as those affecting sight or hearing and learning difficulties.

Definition, causes and types

Definition of Cerebral Palsy

This condition is essentially impairment to the brain. One medical definition is that "cerebral palsy is caused by a brain lesion which is non-progressive and leads to variable impairment of the co-ordination of muscle action, with resulting inability of the person to maintain normal movements. However, it may be the case that as a child gets older their needs may change" (Scope Publications).

Cerebral Palsy can be caused by:

- damage to the brain during pregnancy as a result of infections, such as rubella (German measles)
- during birth, for example by lack of oxygen
- during the first years of life, for example by conditions such as meningitis

Cerebral palsy is not generally considered to be an inherited condition. It can occur in any family, regardless of the age of the mother, social background and origin. Figures within the last five years of the occurrence of cerebral palsy, amount to 2.5 in every 1000 births.

Types of Cerebral Palsy

- **Spastic cerebral palsy** means that muscles feel stiff and are quite difficult to control. Some of the related difficulties are:
  i) Hemiplegia, where either the left or right side of the body is affected by the spasticity but other parts of the body remain unaffected;
  ii) Diplegia, where the legs are affected, but hands are either unaffected or only slightly so;
  iii) Quadriplegia, where the legs and arms are all affected.
- **Athetoid Cerebral Palsy** means the muscles change from being stiff to becoming floppy and movements cannot be controlled. Speech can also be affected, through abnormal movements of tongue and vocal cords.
- **Ataxic Cerebral Palsy** affects balance and hand movements can be shaky; speech development may be slow. Spatial awareness is affected, but walking is possible, if jerky.

The diagrams below illustrate the functions of different areas in the brain

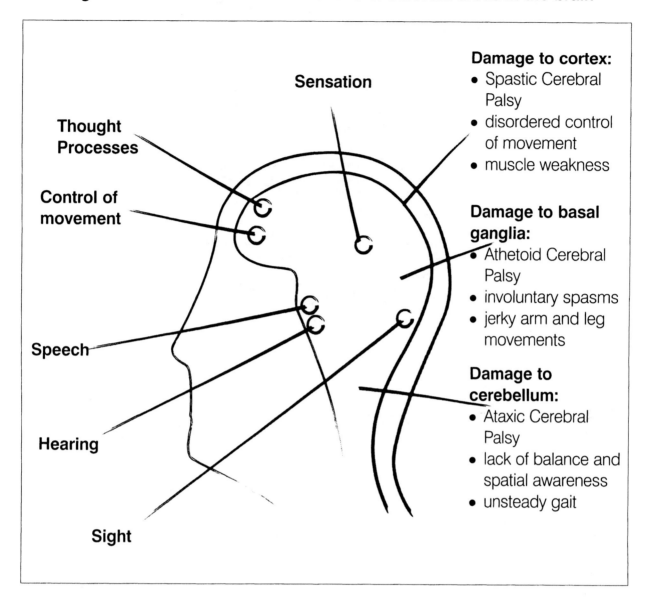

Sensation

Thought Processes

Control of movement

Speech

Hearing

Sight

Damage to cortex:
- Spastic Cerebral Palsy
- disordered control of movement
- muscle weakness

Damage to basal ganglia:
- Athetoid Cerebral Palsy
- involuntary spasms
- jerky arm and leg movements

Damage to cerebellum:
- Ataxic Cerebral Palsy
- lack of balance and spatial awareness
- unsteady gait

- The Cortex (or outer layer of the brain) concerns thought, movement and sensation.

- The Basal Ganglia are situated below the cortex and in the middle of the brain and this area, together with the cerebellum helps to ensure that movement is well organised, graceful and economical.

- The Cerebellum is at the base of the brain and governs functions of the body such as co-ordination of movement, posture and balance. It is linked to the brain stem, which connects the upper brain with the spinal cord.

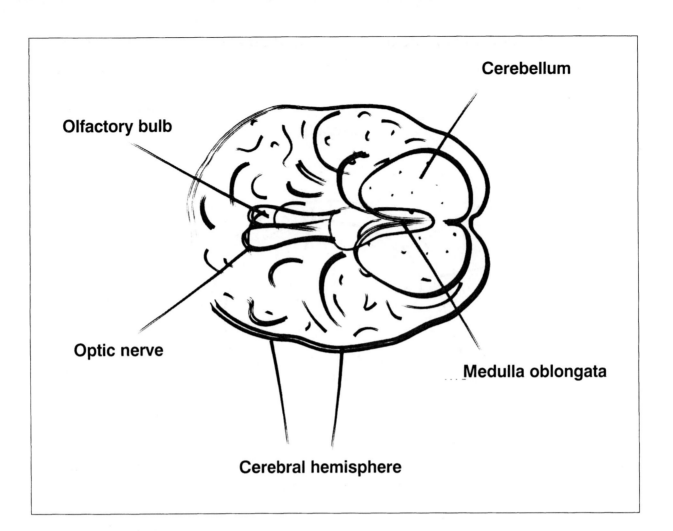

Olfactory bulb

Cerebellum

Optic nerve

Medulla oblongata

Cerebral hemisphere

Part	Function
Olfactory Bulb	Concerned with sense of smell
Optic Nerve	Conveys impulses to optic lobes for sense of sight
Cerebellum	For balance and muscular co-ordination
Medulla Oblongata	Controls automatic reactions, e.g. heart beat, peristalsis, breathing
Cerebral Hemispheres	Controls conscious activity; act as centres for retaining past sensations (memory)
Pituitary	Master gland of endocrine system: produces hormones, regulates other glands

Associated difficulties

Cerebral palsy covers a wide spectrum of needs. It ranges in degree of severity from extreme, including learning disabilities, to very mild, with minimal disabilities.
In other words extreme damage could mean impairments in the following areas;

- hearing
- sight
- speech
- mobility
- co-ordination
- chewing
- swallowing
- digestive difficulties
- epilepsy may also result

N.B. It is important to note that many people with cerebral palsy have average and often above average intelligence even when the level of physical disability is severe.

Emotional issues

Issues which may arise

- the pupil's entitlement to participate in an activity, such as PE or school visits, is not recognised;
- instances of physical and verbal bullying;
- frustration at not being able to participate alongside peers;
- resentment as there is a growing awareness of restrictions the disability brings;
- difficulty in maintaining and sustaining positive peer group relationships.

Approaches to dealing with emotional issues:

- talk about the issues with the pupil;
- ask what they are feeling;
- let the pupil know that it is all right to feel like this at times;
- give reassurance and support.

Strategies and practical help

- Spend time with the pupil. Find a suitable time, just before school, break time, lunchtime, etc. This can take place away from the other pupils, when the member of staff is under less pressure. Let the pupil know that time will be available.
- Endeavour to structure activities to engender an inclusive environment.
- The situation should be monitored and possibly included in the IEP.
- Discuss with the child possible strategies to overcome the difficulties.
- Talk to parents, colleagues, SENCO, CSA, other professionals, e.g. social worker, physiotherapist, medical staff.
- Use circle time in class.
- Use the PSHE sessions.
- Encourage parents to talk about the problem with their children.
- Encourage parents to talk to the teacher and all support agencies, the occupational therapist, advisory support services for pupils with physical difficulties.

Educational implications

The following issues need to be considered by the teacher and the SENCO when establishing how a pupil will be fully included in all school activities:

- Do you have all the relevant information regarding the pupil's needs, e.g. IEPs, statement, Annual Review, reports from physiotherapist, SENSS, advisory support teachers?

- Do you know which agencies are involved with the pupil and the contact personnel, e.g. previous school, health personnel – physiotherapist, occupational therapist, speech and language therapist, school nurse, specialist nurse?

- Does the pupil require any medication to be administered at school?

- Are additional programmes required to meet the pupil's needs? e.g. SALT, physiotherapy, dressing, toileting, fine motor skills, gross motor skills?

- Can the timetable be altered to facilitate movement between lessons?

- Can lessons be timetabled on the ground floor?

Support staff: effective deployment

Not all pupils with cerebral palsy will require additional adult support in order to meet their needs within the classroom. For those pupils who have a more significant level of need, however, the provision of support staff is vital to ensure that their needs can be met.

Teachers may consider the following issues to ensure the most effective deployment of support staff:

- Support staff should promote independence at all times.

- It will not be necessary to work alongside the pupil in every lesson.

- Consider the position of support staff within the classroom.

- Allow the pupil to focus on the teacher, rather than on support staff.

- Support staff should take notes during teacher input in order to reinforce key points at a later stage in the lesson.

- Support staff should monitor and record appropriate information about the pupil, e.g. physical performance, temperament.

- Liaison procedures between home and school should be established under the guidance of the SENCO/head of year/class teacher or form tutor.

- Support staff should work under the direction of the SENCO, class teacher or individual subject teachers.

- In practical sessions when the pupil needs to manipulate specialised equipment, support staff should work under the direction of the pupil.

- Withdrawal of the pupil for physical management routines should be negotiated with the SENCO and individual subject teachers.

> Recognise that the ultimate responsibility for a pupil's access to the curriculum is that of the classroom teacher. Support staff facilitate the delivery of an appropriately differentiated curriculum under the direction of the teacher.

The primary role of support staff is to facilitate independent learning and to enable the pupil to do as much as possible for him/herself. However, there are two further areas which contribute towards supporting a pupil with cerebral palsy.

1. **Physical management:**
- assist with or supervise on-site mobility;
- assist with personal hygiene and cleansing routines;
- supervise in the playground;
- implement exercise programmes overseen by the physiotherapist;
- monitor seating position;
- administer medication;
- check and store specialist equipment;
- assist with feeding;
- operate equipment such as hoists and stairclimbers;
- liaise with outside agencies, e.g. occupational therapist, physiotherapist, school nurse.

2. **Classroom/curricular access:**
- work on a one-to-one basis and in small groups;
- set up equipment;
- note key points;
- take notes/amanuensis;
- verbal prompts;
- organise work sheets and resources;
- support alternative recording strategies, e.g. tape recorder, photocopying notes;
- implement a speech and language programme;
- support access to the curriculum;
- develop self-help skills;
- avoid creating dependency.

Support staff should:

- **have a clear understanding of their roles and responsibilities**
  - have a knowledge of their job description;
  - know that information given to parents should be with the knowledge of the classteacher;
  - respect the confidentiality of information about pupils;
  - maintain a professional demeanour with parents;
  - be aware of school policies with regard to behaviour, anti-bullying, Child Protection, etc.

- **be aware of the channels of communication within school**
  - ensure that information given by parents is relayed to SENCO/classteacher/ form tutor;
  - ensure that communication with outside agencies is carried out in consultation with the SENCO;
  - ensure that there is a mechanism for disseminating information to support staff about school activities, e.g. day book, staff room, notice board.

- **be recognised as valued team members**
  - participate in the planning and monitoring process;
  - celebrate and share their expertise.

- **be encouraged to make use of their personal skills**
  - share skills in the areas of ICT, organisation, creative arts.

- **be supported with appropriate on-going professional development opportunities**
  - observe and learn from other professionals;
  - take advantage of training opportunities in school and relevant external courses.

- **encourage the pupil's independence at all times:**
  - promote independent work habits;
  - promote independent life skills;
  - promote independent play skills.

Support staff: guidelines

Avoid	but instead…
• sitting yourself next to the pupil in class at all times	• work with other pupils, whilst keeping an eye on the pupil you are assigned to
• offering too close an oversight during breaks and lunchtimes	• foster peer group relationships, e.g. a buddy system, introduce games including other pupils
• isolating the pupil by the positioning of any equipment	• ensure the pupil is part of the working group
• assuming that it is your responsibility to collect all equipment for the pupil	• where appropriate, encourage the pupil to organise and be responsible for their own work materials – peer group help is acceptable
• completing the task for the pupil	• ensure that the work is the pupil's – note level of any adult input
• allowing inappropriate age behaviour, e.g. holding a pupil's hand in the playground and the school	• give the minimum of physical assistance to ensure that the pupil is safe and can interact with peers
• making unnecessary allowances for the pupil	• ensure that school rules apply to all
• keeping a pupil in at break and lunchtimes – unless there is specific guidance	• ensure that the pupil takes the opportunity to mix with friends
• making decisions for the pupil	• give the pupil the opportunity to make choices and decisions
• preventing the pupil from taking the consequences of their actions	• insist that the pupil takes the responsibility for and the consequences of their actions
• tolerating inappropriate behaviour such as bad language	• follow the school's behaviour policy

Accessing school and curriculum

Adaptations within the school

1. Has an evaluation of site access requirements been undertaken?
   - entry point, toilet facilities, subject room access, library, dining room, hall.

2. Has an appropriate fire evacuation procedure been established in conjunction with the fire service?

3. Where will the pupil be seated in the classroom and the assembly hall?
   - ensure classroom furniture is arranged to permit maximum access for pupils using aids for mobility such as sticks, wheelchairs, rollators.

4. At breaktimes:
   - provide pupil with a 'buddy' to open doors, gain access to toilet;
   - be aware that static pupils become cold more quickly than those who are more mobile and will need appropriate clothing;
   - have a quiet area for less active pupils to talk;
   - provide alternative options at breaktime for a group of pupils, e.g. tabletop games;
   - allow time for pupils using wheelchairs or mobility equipment to have as full a breaktime as possible, by letting them leave the classroom a few minutes early;
   - have an adult led game in the playground to include pupils who are unsteady or unsure.

5. What happens when the pupil arrives at school?
   - identify entry and departure points.

6. Who is responsible for the pupil on arrival?

7. What level of support is required for issues surrounding on-site mobility?
   - oversight for change of lessons;
   - break and lunchtime supervision.

8. What adult assistance is required for personal hygiene routines?
   - who will provide the advice/training required?

9. What are the contingency arrangements if designated staff are absent?

10. What is the monitoring system?

11. What are the arrangements for ensuring that there is effective home/school communication?

12. How will additional programmes be incorporated into the school day and ensure that the pupil continues to have a broad and balanced curriculum? e.g. try varying the times, so that the same activity is not missed each time.

13. What arrangements need to be made for out of school visits?

   - additional transport requirements, check facilities prior to visit, alternative activity, accessible venue, toilet access, medication.

14. What arrangements are needed for administering medication?

   - storage of medicines, personnel.

15. A variety of equipment may be required to support the pupil in different areas of need, e.g. Stairclimber for taking manual wheelchairs to upper floors, hoist for issues of moving and handling, rollator, manual or powered wheelchair, sticks, ramps, commode chair, adapted seating, perching stool for use in laboratories, modified technology tools, Walkman, word processor, foot blocks, angled boards.

Consider:

- who will determine what equipment is required and who will provide it?
- what training is needed for staff to support the use of this equipment and who will provide the necessary training, e.g. advisory teachers provide training for using stairclimbers, hoists, moving and handling?
- what are the procedures for reporting any repairs and who is responsible for carrying out repairs, e.g. school site manager, wheelchair services, advisory teachers for pupils with physical disablities?
- where will the equipment be stored?
- who will determine when it is to be used?
- additional equipment may require appropriate storage, charging facilities.

Differentiation

The National Curriculum states that it may be necessary to choose "knowledge, skills and understanding from earlier or later key stages… there may not be time to teach all aspects of age related programmes of study." It is important, however, to have high but realistic expectations of pupils.

Differentiation can take place in a number of ways:

1. Consider suggestions in the document 'Including All Children in the Literacy Hour and Daily Mathematics Lesson' (Department for Education and Skills).

2. In the literacy hour, give pupils questions at the appropriate level and give them adequate time to respond, to demonstrate that the answers are valued.

3. The manipulation of small number cards in the Numeracy strategy may be difficult for some pupils. How can you adapt the materials? e.g. Velcro™, Dycem™ (non slip mat), larger squares, bigger counters.

4. Use P scales to find the appropriate level of work (see Kingston upon Hull Target Setting book).

5. Tasks should be broken down into small steps.

6. Materials should be at the pupil's level, e.g. worksheets matching reading level.

7. Use less information on a page with an appropriate size of print or font.

8. Use a pictorial representation of the task, e.g. visual timetable, (see appendix 1). In Numeracy, have a cue card with pictures of pen, ruler, calculator, exercise book so that the pupil knows what to collect. For Literacy, use a prompt card with date, margin, name, etc. so the pupil can start a piece of work without adult assistance and therefore adopt more independent work habits.

9. Information and instructions should be given in appropriate language.

10. Give input to start the pupil in the activity.

11. Avoid copying from the board – provide pre-written notes.

12. Give frequent praise for targets achieved.

13. Supply a list of keywords in advance to support staff, who can then give a brief overview of the main points of the lesson.

14. Consider groupings: collaborative working in pairs or groups will support inclusive activities.

15. Allow time to absorb information, gather materials and complete work.

16. Is a modified PE programme required?

    – Is advice needed from the physiotherapist regarding appropriate activities to be incorporated?

    – Will additional staff be required to support such activities?

17. Recognise the level of effort demanded to enable a pupil to perform a function or carry out a task.

18. Pupils may need assistance with manipulating equipment in Science, Technology and practical areas of the curriculum. Allow the pupil to direct activities if he/she is unable to handle the equipment.

19. Examine what it is that you are assessing, e.g. a pupil's knowledge of a concept rather than his/her reading ability and mark accordingly.

20. Remember the pupil is entitled to the same amount of teacher input as other pupils.

21. Ensure assessments allow pupils to demonstrate their ability by ensuring alternative methods of recording are available.

Alternative recording strategies

Consider the following ideas with pupils who have difficulty in the area of fine motor control, maintaining the pace of recording or coping with the volume of recording required:

- take notes on behalf of the pupil;
- note key points from lesson;
- act as an amanuensis for the pupil who dictates work;
- produce enlarged work sheets;
- use a tape recorder for relevant activities;
- photocopy notes from class teacher or another pupil;
- use an interactive white board;
- set up and position a word processor or lap top;
- alternative computer access devices may be required, e.g. keyguard, alternative keyboard, mouse emulation;
- ensure homework is recorded as necessary in planner, home/school diary;
- use larger squared paper, wider lines;
- consider cloze procedure work which requires the pupil to demonstrate knowledge by filling in blank spaces as necessary.

Teaching dictation skills

For many pupils, i.e. those with moderate to severe cerebral palsy, the most effective means of recording work is by dictation, especially with the increased demands at secondary level. However, dictating work, whether to a support assistant or using word recognition software, requires a level of skill, experience and discipline.

It is important that the support assistant does not anticipate the answer, extend or improve sentences, since the aim is to provide evidence of the pupil's level of attainment. Additionally, to get good grades in examinations pupils need to show the planning of an essay since this can add marks if there is not time to finish a question.

Pupils need to develop a series of skills in the following sequence:

Stage:	To move to the next stage:
The pupil dictates:	
● short phrases;	– discuss redrafting and ask the question who did what/when/where/why;
● longer strings of phrases linked with many 'and's;	– go over work and ask pupil to break it up into shorter sentences based on the above;
● grammatically correct short sentences;	– use set/created Clicker grids to demonstrate links and sentence structure;
	– use 'story starts' and picture sequences to extend sentences;
● longer grammatically correct sentences with one linking word, e.g. and, but, however, although;	– read the pupil's work back and ask him/her to note breath pauses (full stop) and shorter pauses (comma), make it a game;
● sentences knowing when to indicate 'new sentence', 'full stop', 'comma', 'new paragraph'.	– give the pupil a passage with no punctuation and ask him/her to punctuate.
Planning answers, the pupil:	
● can sequence a series of sentences describing an activity;	– use set/prepared Clicker grids;
● can identify the beginning, middle and end of a story;	– give longer passages cut up and ask the pupil to sequence them;
● can plan a short story by giving main points (written on 'Post-its') and organising these into an answer.	– use software e.g. 'Kidspiration', or 'Inspiration' for older pupils, to help the planning process.

Developing concentration

Pupils with cerebral palsy may have difficulty developing concentration skills. The following tables show the stages of development and gives strategies to improve the skill.

Stages of development	Activities to develop concentration
Stage one This is the stage of extreme distractibility. The pupil's attention moves from one object or event to another.	Provide toys to catch the pupil's interest – windmills, bouncing toys, bubbles, squeaky toys, roller ball tracks. Use toys with which the pupil can easily create a reaction. Use toys which require the pupil to follow – a large, noisy car. Rhymes – 'Round and round the garden.'
Stage two The child can concentrate for some time on a concrete task of their own choice. The pupil may not tolerate any intervention in the task in hand and can be very single channelled.	Demonstration by an adult of a toy, allow the pupil to play, extend the pupil's exploration and vocalise action, e.g. posting boxes, building towers of bricks and knocking them down, water play. Use of cause and effect computer programs and cause and effect switched toys. The completion of the tasks makes the reward part of the activity, e.g. form boards.
Stage three Attention is still single channelled but becomes more flexible. The pupil's full attention must be on the directions and immediately transferred to the task. The directions may be verbal or the task may be demonstrated.	Gain attention before giving short instructions. Short tasks with reward given for completion of the task. Give adult support for the task to avoid frustration developing. Matching games, copying patterns with crayons, simple jigsaws, picture books, nesting boxes.
Stage four The pupil has to alternate his full attention between the speaker and the task but he/she does it without the adult needing to focus his attention.	Aim to reduce adult input. Encourage attention to task by comments, 'Well done'. Encourage the pupil to stay on task while listening to the instruction. Build up concentration from a one-to-one situation to larger groups.
Stage five The pupil can assimilate verbal directions without the need to interrupt the task. Pupils at this stage are ready to be taught in a class, where directions are often given to the class while the pupils carry out a task.	The pupil should concentrate with minimal input, i.e. occasional prompts if attention lapses. The pupil should be able to work alongside others.
Stage six This is the mature school level. Integrated attention is well established and well sustained.	The pupil can be introduced to more complex stimuli.

NB The above stages illustrate a normal progression of the stages of concentration. Some pupils will require very structured objectives to achieve progress. Movement from one stage to another may be a very slow process. It is important that the pupil's ability to learn independently is incorporated in the pupil's IEP. Ensure that the objects and tasks are age appropriate.

Developing listening skills

Some pupils with cerebral palsy may have difficulty developing listening skills. The stages of development are linked to the stages in 'Developing concentration'.

Stage 1 When the pupil is extremely distractible. Appropriate activities would be:

- Encourage attention to sounds using activity toys that make noises – rattles, musical toys, jack-in-the-box, wind chimes, spinning tops.
- Sing rhymes to the pupil.

Stage 2 When the pupil is learning to tolerate the adult's presence and involvement in an activity of the pupil's choosing. Appropriate activities would be:

- Encourage attention to sounds with the use of activity toys that make noises – cars with sound effects.
- Use musical instruments – draw attention to the different sounds
- Use action rhymes – 'Ring a roses'.
- Make a choice of two activities "Do you want to paint or do a jigsaw?"
- Ask the pupil to fetch familiar objects: "Find your coat," etc.

Stage 3 The pupil is beginning to control his/her focus of attention. Suitable activities would be:

- Ask for objects, e.g "Show me the lion", using miniature toys or pictures.
- Sing nursery rhymes and songs and leave a pause for the child to supply the missing word. Play musical statues.

- Read familiar stories, with repetitive lines for the child to join in, e.g. The Three Little Pigs.
- Read a story on an individual basis. Ask the pupil to hold up a toy animal when he/she hears the name of the animal in the story.

Stage 4 The pupil is beginning to transfer attention skills to the group. Suitable activities would be:

- Match sounds to objects or pictures.
- Tell a story with a child's name in it. Ask the pupil to put his/her hand up when he/she hears their name.
- Ask for objects, build up the number of objects in the sequence, e.g. put objects in a shopping bag.
- Follow simple commands – ask the pupil to touch two or three body parts.

Stage 5 The pupil is transferring attention to the classroom situation. Suggestions for activities:

- Play Simple Simon Says.
- Read a story, give the pupils pictures to hold up when they hear the name of the article on the picture.
- The pupils sit in a circle. When a name is called, the bean bag is thrown to that pupil.

Developing visual perception

Visual perception is the ability to interpret or give meaning to what is seen.
Pupils with cerebral palsy may have problems with visual perception. This may cause significant difficulties that the following suggestions may overcome:

- build up simple routines;
- tidy a work area before the start of a new task;
- mark an area of personal workspace for a pupil to have boundaries within which to work, without spreading into his/her neighbour's space;
- use cards with cues (visual or written) to help the organisation of a task;
- use cues (visual or written) to help structure the timetable for a whole or part of a day (see appendix 1);
- keep articles required for different subjects in transparent wallets to facilitate clear identification;
- have storage areas in the classroom clearly labelled with a picture and/or written label to aid the collection and storage of equipment;
- provide support for new pupils to a school (buddy system) to enable the pupil to familiarise him/herself with the new layout of the building or site;
- use a diary to enable the pupil to organise him/herself for PE, homework;
- use a visual guide when reading, e.g. a piece of card, finger;
- support the development of dressing skills by encouraging the pupil to lay out his/her clothes neatly, put them in a pile in the order which they were removed and have clothes with logos, etc. to identify the back/front, use picture cues to give the order of dressing;
- give information in small sections (one instruction at a time with a gradual build up);
- give pupils opportunities to talk through activities;
- avoid placing pupils next to distractions, e.g. windows, a busy corridor, a bright display;
- create worksheets with a minimum of information and avoid distracting detail.

Developing self-esteem

Self-esteem begins to build up as a consequence of our interaction with other people. Cooley (1962) said that we form our self-image from the feedback we receive from 'significant others'. For the pupil with cerebral palsy in school, the significant others are teachers and other staff and their peers. They can have a powerful effect on the development of the pupil's self image. High or low levels of self-esteem can affect how an individual faces new challenges and influence his/her feelings as a learner, towards school, peers and his/her future.

The following strategies may help to build self-esteem:

- make all goals attainable;
- set work at the appropriate level;
- observe any difficulties the pupil has, and by task analysis, teach the elements;
- recognise that the pupil's contribution to the school community is valuable;
- recognise that progress may take place in small steps and reward success, academic or otherwise, appropriately;
- display the pupil's work alongside his/her peers;
- acknowledge the pupil's strengths – politeness, kindness, perseverance;
- have feedback sessions at the end of a lesson which include an element of success;
- ensure all staff are aware of the pupil's difficulties and support in the necessary way;
- encourage the pupil to make contributions to his/her IEP and to be a part of the review process;
- celebrate the pupil's success with their parents.

Positive peer group relationships

In the classroom:

- ensure that adults value the pupil and other pupils will follow by example;

- provide useful jobs that pupils with cerebral palsy and their peers can share;

- give the pupil space; supporting adults should step back and allow friendships to flourish;

- ensure the pupil with cerebral palsy has access to the same activities as their peers, although differentiated and adapted activities may be necessary;

- ensure classroom activities are jointly accessible to pupils with cerebral palsy and their peers.

At break time:

- allow time for pupils with unsteady gait or equipment to aid mobility, to have a full break time; consider the help the pupil needs to get to the playground;

- provide the pupil with a 'buddy' to open doors, push the wheelchair, gain access to the toilet;

- ensure toileting routines do not prevent pupils from mixing with their peers;

- provide alternative options at playtime for a group of pupils – table-top games, construction toys;

- have a coned area for football, etc. to protect pupils who are vulnerable because of an unsteady gait;

- have an adult-led game in the playground to include pupils who are unsteady or a wheelchair user in the playground;

- have quiet areas for less active play for pupils to share conversation;

- provide adapted equipment for pupils in wheelchairs, e.g. soft balls to allow them to play with their peers;

- be aware that pupils may be subject to verbal and/or physical bullying related to their condition, and that staff need to respond accordingly.

Effective home–school liaison

Parents hold key information and have a critical role to play in their children's education. In order to create a good relationship the following suggestions are made:

- Parents should be aware of the Code of Practice and its implications for them.
- They should have an understanding of the stages within the Code and know which stage their child is at.
- Parents should be invited to contribute to IEPs, attend review meetings and discuss how they can support the IEP.
- Provide reports for parents before annual reviews.
- Parents should know who to contact if they have concerns about their child, for example:
  - classteacher
  - SENCO
  - headteacher
  - Special Needs Governor.
- Parental concerns should be listened to and acknowledged.
- Parents should be trusted as partners.
- Parents may be encouraged to become involved in the life of the school, e.g. as reading partners, helpers on school trips.
- Ensure parents are informed of visits from other professionals, e.g. Educational Psychologist, Physiotherapist.
- Consult parents before changes in provision are made.
- Use a home/school diary to allow school and home to create a dialogue about what the child is doing.
- Celebrate success, large or small, with parents.

Individual Education Plans

The following pen pictures illustrate the range of needs of pupils with cerebral palsy, from the mild to the severe end of the continuum. Some pupils will require an Individual Education Plan (IEP) to meet their needs. These should include SMART targets: Small, Measurable, Achievable, Realistic, with timescales. Timescales should be set for review of the targets and consideration given to the need for new ones. It is important that pupils are involved in the writing of their own targets. Parents should also involved be in the setting and reviewing of targets and be encouraged to carry out activities at home which support the targets.

Other pupils will require a physical management programme, devised in conjunction with the physiotherapist, SENCO and advisory support teachers. This should maximise opportunities; e.g. a standing frame could be used when other pupils are standing in science lessons; exercises can be incorporated into warm-up activities in PE.

Paul

Paul is a happy 5-year-old child in the Reception class who has spastic diplegia, which affects both lower limbs. He is ambulant but has an unsteady gait and poor saving responses (cannot steady himself or save himself from falling). He wears ankle foot orthoses (shaped supports). He needs adult supervision for on-site mobility. He uses a wheelchair to negotiate long distances. He has a physical management programme (exercises which take place daily), which is devised and overseen by the physiotherapist and implemented by support staff in school. Paul has a speech and language delay but is keen to communicate with both peers and adults. His speech is unclear to adults with whom he is not familiar. He has recently established independent toileting routines, but he requires minimal adult oversight for adjusting his clothes and for safety on wet surfaces. He can use a spoon and fork to eat independently. He is able to dress his upper body if he is wearing loose-fitting clothing, but has some difficulty in putting on his trousers, socks and shoes. He will attempt to copy the letters of his name, but they are large and poorly formed.

Louise

Louise is a Year 6 pupil who has cerebral palsy affecting all four limbs and her ability to speak. She is a popular girl who is out-going and confident. She shares the same interests as many girls of her age and goes horse riding and loves her pets. Louise uses a range of mobility aids including a powered wheelchair, a manual wheelchair and a walking frame. When using the powered chair, Louise is able to move around the school site over level surfaces and gentle inclines, independently. She requires assistance with opening doors and carrying her equipment. Louise is able to weight-bear when transferring between chairs and when using her walker. In the primary school setting, Louise uses a manual wheelchair with a supportive seating insert. This wheelchair fits on a stair climber to take Louise to the classrooms on the first floor.

Louise uses a Pathfinder™ (a communication aid which uses synthesised speech) to communicate verbally. She also uses a range of gestures and facial expressions which clearly convey meaning and can be easily interpreted in context. In addition, Louise uses a range of 'low tech' strategies to communicate. These are computer-generated word or symbol boards, prepared by the support assistant in conjunction with recommendations made by the Speech and Language Therapist. Louise can become frustrated by her communication difficulties but this has improved since she started using the Pathfinder™. Louise has a complex communication disorder. However, her listening and comprehension skills are within age-appropriate limits.

Louise enjoys using pencils and crayons and can hold these in her left hand and colour objects with increasing accuracy. She can write her name but realistically, writing by hand will never be a viable method of recording for her. Louise uses a PC laptop with a keyguard and a specialist joystick. She uses standard software alongside specialist software which supports her communication needs. The Pathfinder™ communication aid also has a cut-down version of a Windows program and can be used for word processing. However, this involves changing the keyboard overlay which is a slow process. It is possible to download conversations from the Pathfinder™ to a PC computer.

Louise requires support in all lessons which involve the manipulation of resources and recording written work. Her work output speed is considerably slower than her peers'. Louise requires assistance with all dressing and undressing; she requires assistance to eat and drink. Louise is totally continent but requires adult support to transfer to the toilet, adjust her clothing and deal with cleansing. She requires access to a spacious toilet facility where support can be given in privacy.

Louise does not have significant learning needs so does not require an IEP for learning issues. However, she does have a timetable which illustrates the support she needs to access the curriculum.

The following pages show an IEP to meet Paul's needs and a timetable to indicate the support required for Louise to access the curriculum.

Primary School

Name: Paul
Date: 12. 3. 04

Date of birth: 4. 9. 99
Review Date: 20. 6. 04

Nature of pupil's difficulties: Difficulty putting on lower garments after PE. Inability to form letters appropriately. Difficulty using scissors appropriately.

Targets	Strategies	Resources	Evaluation
To put on socks independently	Teach through backward chaining, i.e. 1. Pull sock on over heel, Paul to pull sock up. 2. Put sock over instep, Paul to pull over heel. 3. Put sock onto toe, Paul to pull up. 4. Paul to put sock on with verbal prompts.	Practise with large sized socks.	
To form a pattern of letters correctly (c, o, a, d)	Making large letter formations in the air. Overwriting letters in varied media. Overwriting/writing letters with various media, reduce letter sizes.	Foam, sand, finger paint. Chalk, felt tip pens, paint, triangular pencils.	
To cut along a wavy line	Cut between 2 slightly curved lines. Increase the bends in the lines. Decrease the gaps between the lines. Cut along a thick black wavy line.	Cutting sheets (card). Specialist scissors (spring scissors).	

Primary School

Name:

Date:

Date of birth:

Review Date:

Nature of pupil's difficulties:

Targets	Strategies	Resources	Evaluation

A timetable to show how additional adult support is used to facilitate access to the curriculum for Louise

		Numeracy strategy (equipment required)	Assembly	Break	Literacy hour (equipment required)	Lunch	Afternoon sessions (equipment required)	Break	Afternoon sessions (equipment required)
Monday	SALT work	Use of Pathfinder™ Communication Aid	Standing transfer to standard classroom		Pathfinder™ Communication Aid		**Technology** spring loaded scissors non slip mat	Louise free sitting during guided reading	**History** Symbol board
Tuesday	Physiotherapy	PC Laptop with keyguard and joystick			PC Laptop with keyboard and joystick		**Geography** Symbol board		**RE** Symbol board
Wednesday	SALT work	100 square grid					**PE** physiotherapy in warm up, differentiated activities		**Science** adapted equipment
Thursday	SALT work	X grid					**PE** physiotherapy in warm up, differentiated activities		**ICT** PC laptop with keyguard
Friday	SALT work	(any other maths equipment as requested)					**Music** PC laptop		**ART** spring loaded scissors non slip mat

Charge electrical equipment as necessary

Support staff assist with/supervise: ● on-site mobility; ● positioning and assisting with the manipulation of equipment; ● oversight for break and lunchtime; ● assist with personal hygiene routines; ● implement physical management routines; ● implement speech and language (SALT) routines.

Glossary

Amanuensis	A person who scribes for a pupil
EP	Educational Psychologist
IEP	Individual Education Plan
ICT	Information and Communication Technology
INSET	In-service Training
LEA	Local Education Authority
Orthoses	A piece of equipment to correct, prevent or support a fully or partially correctible malformation
OT	Occupational Therapist – someone who assesses and makes recommendations to enable the pupil to function more effectively
Physiotherapist	A person who assesses and makes recommendations for the pupil regarding posture, muscle tone and mobility
PSHE	Personal Social and Health Education
SALT	Speech and Language Therapy
Saving responses	Actions taken to steady oneself, save from a fall
SENCO	Special Educational Needs Co-ordinator
SENSS	Special Educational Needs Support Service
Orthotist	A person who assesses and provides splints and appliances
Stairclimber	A mechanism for moving a wheelchair up stairs.
Rollator	Equipment to facilitate independent walking

Acknowledgements and useful contacts

Clicker 4
SEMERC
Granada Learning Ltd
Granada Television, Quay Street
Manchester M60 9EA
www.semerc.com

Cooke and Williams (1985)
Language Development and Assessment
Winslow Press

Fox, G. (1998)
A Handbook for Learning Support Assistance
(teachers and assistants working together)
David Fulton

Including All Children in the Literacy Hour and Daily Mathematics Lesson
Department for Education and Skills
DfES 0465/2002

Index for Inclusion CSIE
Booth, T., Ainscow, M., Black-Hawkins,
K., Vaughan, M., Shaw, L. (2000)

Kingston upon Hull Target Setting book
Learning Services
Essex House, Manor Road
Kingston upon Hull HU1 1YD
Tel: 01482 613423

Male, J. (1997)
Children First
RADAR

Nottingham Rehab Supplies
Findell Educational Ltd
Findell House
Excelsior Road, Ashby Park
Ashby de la Zouch
Leicester LE65 1NG
Tel: 0845 1204522

Number games
Trackerballs
Ready for writing
SEMERC
Granada Learning Ltd
Granada Television, Quay Street
Manchester M60 9EA
www.semerc.com

SCOPE (1999)
Cerebral Palsy
SCOPE Publications (London)

Write from the Start
Ion Teodorescu and Lois Addy
LDA
Duke St, Wisbech
Cambs PE13 2AC
Tel: 01945 46344
www.instructionalfair.co.uk

Useful contacts

SCOPE
6 Market Road
London N7 9PW
Tel: 020 7619 7100

Unit B
Moor Park Business Centre
Thornes Moor Road
Wakefield WF2 8PF
Tel: 01924 366711
Email: northeastandyorkshire@scope.org.uk
Internet: www.scope.org.uk

Prentke Romich International Ltd (Pathfinder)
Minerva House
Minerva Business Park
Lynchwood
Peterborough PE2 6FT

Appendix 1

Timetable   **Name:**   **Form:**

	Monday	Tuesday	Wednesday	Thursday	Friday
1					
2					
3					
4					
5					
6					

These images have been produced by the pupils of Priory Primary School, Hull.

This page may be freely photocopied.

These are whole school issues to be considered by the Senior Management Team when planning to meet the needs of a pupil with cerebral palsy

Consideration	✔	X	Action
Are the governors aware of their responsibilities in ensuring that the needs of the pupil are met?			
Is the building fully accessible for the child?			
Are all staff aware of the educational implications of Cerebral Palsy?			
Is there any additional adult support for the child?			
Are staff appropriately trained?			
Is there effective communication between home and school?			
Are other agencies involved in meeting the needs of the child?			
Do you know where to seek further information and advice?			
Are you aware of recent legislation, LEA/SEN policies?			
Are there strategies to support the child's emotional well-being?			
Are there strategies to promote positive peer group relationships?			
Do you promote positive images of the child?			
Is the curriculum sufficiently differentiated?			
Are any additional resources required to support curriculum delivery?			

Appendix 3: Some professionals who may be involved

Professional	Personnel and contact number
Educational Psychologist	
Special Educational Needs Support Service	
Educational Service for Physical Disability	
Speech and Language Therapist	
Educational Service for the Visually Impaired	
Educational Service for the Hearing Impaired	
Senior Clinical Medical Officer (SCMO)	
School Nurse	
Physiotherapist	
Occupational Therapist	
Paediatric Specialist Nurse	
Support Groups	